Usborne

Little First Stickers
Chinese New Year

Illustrated by BlueBean

You'll find all the stickers at the back of the book.

Words by Amy Chiu and Kristie Pickersgill

Designed by Kirsty Tizzard

Expert advice from Evelyn Ong

At the market

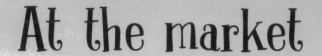

It's almost Lunar New Year in China. Jing and her family are going to the market to buy some decorations. Can you add them to this scene?

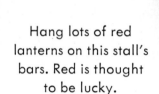

Hang lots of red lanterns on this stall's bars. Red is thought to be lucky.

Find some people buying an orange tree.

Put some people up here decorating their homes.

Add bunches of bright flowers to this stall.

新年快乐
福

3

Getting ready

There are many jobs to do to get ready for New Year. Help Jing and her family by adding lots of decorations around the house.

Stick some lucky bamboo here. It's thought to bring growth and success.

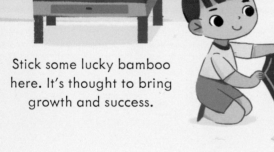

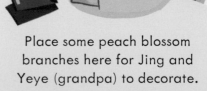

Place some peach blossom branches here for Jing and Yeye (grandpa) to decorate.

In the kitchen

The kitchen is full of tasty smells as food for tonight's big meal is cooking. Friends and family who visit over the next few days might get a snack too!

Nainai (grandma) is making dumplings. Add some more people to help her.

Find Jing's uncle and cousin to do the important job of cleaning. They are sweeping away the past to welcome a new, better year.

Time to eat

Jing's family have gathered together for a delicious New Year's Eve meal. The dishes are specially chosen to bring good luck for the next year.

Pak choi (Chinese cabbage)

Poached chicken, cut and served whole.

Find a plate of spring rolls. These are chosen because they look like gold bars.

Boiled prawns

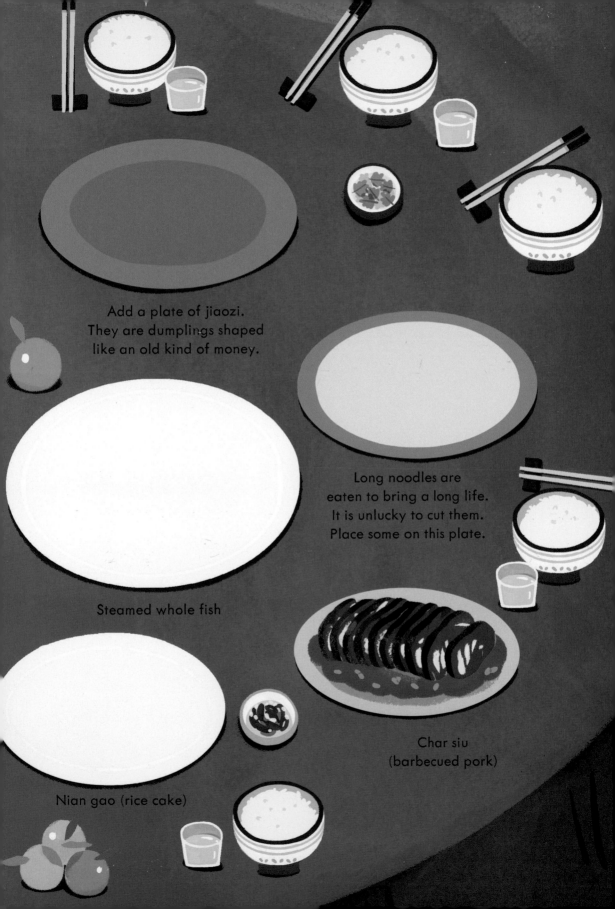

Add a plate of jiaozi.
They are dumplings shaped
like an old kind of money.

Long noodles are
eaten to bring a long life.
It is unlucky to cut them.
Place some on this plate.

Steamed whole fish

Char siu
(barbecued pork)

Nian gao (rice cake)

Fireworks

At midnight, sparkling fireworks fill
the night sky with flashes and bangs.
The loud noises are to scare away
a mythical monster called Nian.

Stick Jing and her
family here playing
with sparklers.

Add some stalls
selling hot food
and drinks.

Dancing dragon

It's New Year's Day! Drums rumble and cymbals crash as the dragon dance begins. The longer the dragon, the more luck it brings for the year ahead.

Put another drummer here.

Find someone with a ball for the dragon to chase.

Dragons represent the Chinese Emperor – strict, kind and wise.
Add lots more dancers to move the powerful dragon.

11

Leaping lions

Now it's time for the lion dance. The lions move playfully to the beat of the drum and make daring leaps between tiny platforms.

Find a red lion to dance with this one.

Stick a brave lion balancing up here.

Lions represent strength.
Add a lively lion prancing
about here.

Glowing lanterns

Chinese New Year celebrations carry on for fifteen days. The very last night is the Lantern Festival. The lanterns are symbols of good luck and hope for the new year.

Add a huge glowing dragon floating on the water.

Stick some lanterns here to light up the sky.

These lanterns have puzzles hanging underneath. Find some people to solve the puzzles.

The Zodiac

In the Chinese calendar, each year is linked to one of 12 animals. Find a sticker to match each of the shapes below.

2023 – Year of the Rabbit
2024 – Year of the Dragon
2025 – Year of the Snake
2026 – Year of the Horse

Rat

Ox

Tiger

Rabbit

Dragon

Snake

Horse

Goat

Monkey

Rooster

Dog

Pig

At the market

Lanterns

Decorating

Flowers

Sugar animals

Food stall

Stallholder

Jing's family

Orange tree

Jing and brother

Getting ready page 4

Sweets

Decorations

Lucky fish

Peach blossom

Lucky knot

Jing

Bamboo

Making lanterns

In the kitchen page 5

Oranges

Dumplings

Making dumplings

Sweeping

Jiaozi (dumplings)

Dips

Boiled prawns

Chopsticks

Steamed whole fish

Noodles

Oranges

Tea

Nian gao
(rice cake)

Pak choi (Chinese cabbage)

Spring rolls

Fireworks

Fireworks

Hot food stalls

Jing and family

Dancing dragon pages 10-11

Crowd

Drummer

Dancer
with ball

Dragon head

Dancers

Leaping lions pages 12–13

Balancing lions

Band

Crowd

Dancing lions

Glowing lanterns pages 14-15

Lanterns

Lantern
puzzles

Water lanterns